Nonprofit Startup Planner

FULL CIRCLE NONPROFIT GROUP

KRISTEN B. VINCENT, MBA

BUSINESS IDEAS

"The best way to predict the future is to create it." - Abraham Lincoln

LIKES

PASSIONS

SKILLS

TALENTS

TARGET MARKET

FULL CIRCLE NONPROFIT GROUP

CHOOSING A NAME

THE BEST WAY TO PREDICT THE FUTURE IS TO CREATE IT - ABRAHAM LINCOLN

ACTION WORDS

DESCRIPTIVE WORDS

THREE IMPORTANT QUESTIONS

FINDING YOUR NONPROFIT'S NICHE

MY NONPROFIT WILL?
• • • • • • • • • • • • • • • • • • • •

MY NONPROFIT HELPS?
• • • • • • • • • • • • • • • • • •

OUR MEMBERS ARE?
• • • • • • • • • • • • • • • • • • •

MARKET RESEARCH

FINDING YOUR NONPROFIT'S NICHE

WHAT MAKES MY NONPROFIT DIFFERENT?

FULL CIRCLE
NONPROFIT GROUP

CHARITABLE PURPOSE

WHAT NEEDS DO I WANT MY CHARITABLE ORGANIZATION TO FULFILL WITHIN THE COMMUNITY?

• • • • • • • • • • • • • • • • • • • •

MISSION STATEMENT

ARTICULATES AN ORGANIZATION'S PURPOSE

WHAT DOES MY NONPROFIT DO?

HOW DOES MY NONPROFIT DO IT?

WHY DOES MY NONPROFIT DO IT?

VISION STATEMENT

ANCHOR POINT TO ANY STRATEGIC PLAN

WHAT ARE MY NONPROFIT'S VALUES?

WHAT IS THE FOCUS OF MY NONPROFIT?

WHAT IS MY STRATEGIC OBJECTIVE?

WHAT ARE THE GOALS OF THE NONPROFIT?

FULL CIRCLE NONPROFIT GROUP

EXECUTIVE SUMMARY

OVERALL SNAPSHOT OF WHAT YOUR VISION IS

WRITE IT SO THAT SOMEONE WHO HAD NEVER HEARD OF YOU WOULD UNDERSTAND WHAT YOU'RE DOING.

• • • • • • • • • • • • • • • •

PROBLEM AND SOLUTION

OVERALL SNAPSHOT OF WHAT YOUR VISION IS

DESCRIBE THE PROBLEM THAT NEEDS TO BE SOLVED FOR YOUR CLIENTS OR YOUR COMMUNITY AT LARGE. THEN SAY HOW YOUR ORGANIZATION SOLVES THE PROBLEM.

• • • • • • • • • • • • • • • • • •

MARKET ANALYSIS WITH A DONOR OR FUNDING FOCUS

THINK ABOUT FUNDING

HOW YOU PLAN TO FUND YOUR PROGRAM, AND WHO WILL USE YOUR SERVICES.

TARGET SUPPORTERS

KNOWING YOUR MONEY COMES FROM

WHO ARE YOUR SUPPORTERS? WHAT KIND OF PERSON DONATES TO YOUR ORGANIZATION?

TARGET CLIENT POPULATION

CLIENTS OF A SPECIFIC PRODUCT OR SERVICE

DEMOGRAPHICS

NOTES:

PSYCHOGRAPHICS

NOTES:

LOCATION AND AVAILABILITY

NOTES:

FULL CIRCLE NONPROFIT GROUP

THE COMPETITION
WHAT YOUR PROSPECTIVE CLIENTS ARE DOING ABOUT THEIR PROBLEM

WHO ARE MY COMPETITORS?

FUTURE PRODUCTS
AND SERVICES

TALK ABOUT LONG-TERM GOALS

WHERE DO YOU WANT TO BE IN FIVE YEARS?

STRATEGIES AND FUNDING AND PROMOTION

MARKETING AND SALES STRATEGIES

HOW ARE YOU GOING TO REACH YOUR TARGET FUNDING SOURCES (DONORS, FOUNDATIONS)?

● ●

HOW ARE YOU GOING TO REACH YOUR TARGET CLIENT POPULATION?

● ● ● ● ● ● ● ● ● ● ● ● ● ● ● ● ● ●

POSITIONING STATEMENT

IDENTIFYING AN APPROPRIATE MARKET NICHE FOR A PRODUCT/SERVICE

HERE'S A BASIC TEMPLATE FOR WRITING A POSITIONING STATEMENT:

● ● ● ● ● ● ● ● ● ● ● ● ● ● ● ● ● ● ●

For [insert Target Market], the [insert Brand] is the [insert Point of Differentiation] among all [insert Frame of Reference] because [insert Reason to Believe]

Example: For World Wide Web users who enjoy books, Amazon.com is a retail bookseller that provides instant access to over 1.1 million books. Unlike traditional book retailers, Amazon.com provides a combination of extraordinary convenience, low prices, and comprehensive selection.

MY POSITIONING STATEMENT

● ● ● ● ● ● ● ● ● ● ● ● ● ● ● ● ● ● ●

COSTS AND FEES

HOW MUCH DOES IT COST FOR PRODUCT AND SERVICE

HOW WILL THE PROGRAM BE FUNDED?

• • • • • • • • • • • • • • • • • • • •

PROMOTION AND RESEARCH

ADVERTISING, PUBLIC RELATIONS, DIGITAL MARKETING

HOW WILL I REACH MY CLIENTS?

STRATEGIC ALLIANCE AND PARTNERSHIP

HOW YOU'LL WORK WITH OTHER ORGANIZATIONS

WHAT ORGANIZATIONS CAN WE PARTNER WITH?

MILESTONES AND METRICS

INDICATORS THAT YOUR PROGRAM IS WORKING

Milestones are Key to Management

• • • • • • • • • • • • • • • •

EVERY BUSINESS MILESTONE SHOULD INCLUDE:

**- A DESCRIPTION OF THE TASK
- A DUE DATE
- A BUDGET
- A RESPONSIBLE PERSON**

3 TYPES OF MILESTONES

• • • • • • • • • • • • • • • •

WHEN YOU'RE BUILDING AND GROWING A BUSINESS, YOU SHOULD END UP SCHEDULING THREE DIFFERENT TYPES OF MILESTONES:

- PLAN REVIEW
- ASSUMPTIONS VALIDATION
- IMPLEMENTATION

PLAN REVIEW

SETS ASIDE TIME TO REVIEW YOUR BUSINESS STRATEGY, TACTICS, FORECAST AND BUDGET

BUSINESS STRATEGY

• • • • • • • • • • • • • •

TACTICS

• • • • • • • • • • • • • •

FORECAST

• • • • • • • • • • • • •

BUDGET

• • • • • • • • • • • •

MILESTONES TO VALIDATE YOUR ASSUMPTIONS

FIGURING OUT IF YOU'VE GOT THE RIGHT STRATEGY

SOME EXAMPLE MILESTONES MIGHT BE:

- INTERVIEW 15 POTENTIAL CLIENTS IN MY PRIMARY MARKET SEGMENT

- RESEARCH PRODUCTS/SERVICES FOR MY COMPETITORS

- CREATE SAMPLE BROCHURE FOR MY NONPROFIT AND SEE WHAT POTENTIAL CLIENTS THINK

● ●

_____

_____

_____

_____

_____

_____

IMPLEMENTING YOUR STRATEGY

CREATE IMPLEMENTATION MILESTONES

THESE ARE THE TASKS YOU'RE GOING TO DO TO ACTUALLY BUILD YOUR BUSINESS. YOU'LL BE DOING THINGS LIKE BUILDING YOUR PRODUCT, SETTING UP YOUR OFFICE OR SHOP, DEVELOPING YOUR WEBSITE

• •

SOME EXAMPLES OF IMPLEMENTATION MILESTONES MIGHT BE:

- NEGOTIATE A LEASE FOR OFFICE SPACE
- DEVELOP A WEB SITE
- BUILD VERSION 1 OF THE PRODUCT
- DEVELOP MARKETING MATERIALS

_____

_____

_____

_____

_____

_____

FULL CIRCLE NONPROFIT GROUP

MANAGEMENT TEAM AND COMPANY
WHO WILL RUN THE NONPROFIT

WHO IS GOING TO BE INVOLVED AND WHAT ARE THEIR DUTIES?
● ● ● ● ● ● ● ● ● ● ● ● ● ● ● ● ● ● ● ●

WHAT DO THESE INDIVIDUALS BRING TO THE TABLE?
● ● ● ● ● ● ● ● ● ● ● ● ● ● ● ● ● ● ●

FINANCIAL PLAN

IT'S ALL ABOUT FUTURE PLANNING

WHAT WILL BE DONE WITH THE SURPLUS?

● ● ● ● ● ● ● ● ● ● ● ● ● ● ● ● ● ●

WHAT WILL YOU DO IF YOU DON'T MEET YOUR FUNDRAISING GOALS?

● ● ● ● ● ● ● ● ● ● ● ● ● ● ● ● ● ●

ARE YOU ACCOUNTING FOR APPROPRIATE AMOUNTS GOING TO PAYROLL AND ADMINISTRATIVE COSTS OVER TIME?

● ● ● ● ● ● ● ● ● ● ● ● ● ● ● ●

RECAP

BUSINESS IS ONGOING

STARTING A NONPROFIT ORGANIZATION CAN BE AN INSPIRING WAY TO HELP THOS IN NEED AS WELL AS GIVE BACK TO YOUR COMMUNITY.

NOTE THAT IT IS IMPORTANT TO UNDERSTAND ALL OF THE STEPS INVOLVED IN THIS PROCESS BEFORE MOVING FORWARD.

GROWING AND SUSTAINING A NONPROFIT SOMETIMES TAKES YEARS OF EFFORT AND A LOTS OF COMMITMENT AND DETERMINATION.

• •

Good Luck!!

Made in the USA
Monee, IL
30 August 2019